CHISWICK AS IT WAS

**A selection of Victorian and early 20th-century photographs
compiled and annotated**

by

**London Borough of Hounslow, Department of Arts and Recreation,
Libraries Division**

and

The Brentford and Chiswick Local History Society

Front cover: The High Road looking towards Young's Corner from Chiswick Lane *c.*1910
(see *Photograph No. 15*).

Inside front cover: A section of the Ordnance Survey Map, 2nd edition 1894–6.
Scale 6″ to 1 mile

First edition – October 1986
Second impression – October 1993

Published by: Hendon Publishing Co. Ltd., Hendon Mill, Nelson, Lancashire.
Printed by Peter Fretwell & Sons Ltd., Goulbourne Street, Keighley, West Yorkshire BD21 1PZ.

INTRODUCTION

Chiswick is today's name for the whole area between Hammersmith and Brentford, but 150 years ago (when photography was a new craft) there were at least five separate places within the parish of St Nicholas. The church had been built on the highest piece of land by the river, and around it grew the village of Chiswick. Turnham Green was another village altogether, one which had grown up on the network of roads between London and the west of England. Strand on the Green was a riverside village similar to Chiswick, and there were two hamlets in the parish, Little Sutton and Stamford Brook. The photographs in this book can give us some idea of how these places were changed into the Chiswick we know today.

We should not think of these places as quiet rural backwaters being suddenly overwhelmed by the house-building that made today's suburb. By the middle of the 19th century there was a surprising amount of industrial activity, especially along the waterfront. Two large breweries, many shipbuilding and barge repair yards, malthouses, stonemasons, papermaking and printing, timber yards, steam laundries, wharves and draw docks unloading heavy goods (especially coal) — all these kept both Chiswick and Strand on the Green busy and noisy places. Things must have taken a turn for the worse when steel replaced wood for the building of boats and barges!

One hundred and fifty years ago about half the parish was cultivated land, either as market gardens or as meadow and pasture. Near to the High Road there was a patchwork of small market gardens and orchards — intensively managed, using a lot of labour and regularly sending cart-loads of produce to market.

Along the High Road itself you would have seen a number of very large town houses — three-, sometimes four-storey buildings with stables and a coach-house, set on a substantial plot of land with walls and gates. Built from the late 17th century onwards, by the mid-19th century many of them were no longer homes for families with servants but had become schools. Their names survive in the estates built after their demolition: Annandale, Linden, Arlington, Belmont, Heathfield, Stile Hall.

Dominating the centre of the parish was the landholding of the Dukes of Devonshire. Since the middle of the 18th century when this family inherited Chiswick House it had bought adjacent properties (Sutton Court, Corney House, Grove House, Sir Stephen Fox's House and Heathfield House) and had enclosed and extinguished the common rights over the large common field south of the High Road. By the mid-19th century it owned nearly half the parish and decisions made by this family and its advisors (how much land to release, what type of housing to allow) had a major impact on the shape and appearance of today's suburb.

Although these villages and hamlets had been growing and expanding (the population had doubled in the fifty years after 1800) the process of suburban house-building which started in the 1860s brought changes on a scale that was wholly new. The census of 1931 recorded the highest number of people living in Chiswick — 42,000. In the middle of the 19th century there were only 6,300. (For comparison, the 1981 census recorded just under 30,000). As the families moved in, so did the shops, service industries and transport facilities. Slowly the 'centre of gravity' of the parish moved from the river to the High Road; symbolic of this change was the decision of the Vestry in 1876 to build their new Hall (later the Town Hall) at Turnham Green, not near St Nicholas Church on the Mall. The High Road developed into the major shopping street of the area, along with Turnham Green Terrace and Devonshire Road. In the present century, while Chiswick Mall and Strand on the Green have lost most of their industrial and commercial elements, the village of Turnham Green has been subject to continuing change.

It is hard for us today to understand how this rapid process of change affected the thoughts and feelings of the people who lived in Chiswick then. But there is one clue which lies in the photographs themselves. Most of the photographs in this book were taken after the introduction of the 'dry plate' in the 1870s, the convenience of which allowed many more people to become amateur photographers. Many of the most useful of the photographs which have since been collected by Chiswick Library are plain 'record' photographs, taken by someone (usually unknown to us) who was aware that a building or an area was about to be demolished and changed.

Since the time these photographs were made Chiswick has changed. Its local government was merged, first with Brentford, then with other neighbouring parishes to form the borough of Hounslow. Its position on the road and river routes out of London, which for so long had been a source of its income, has now worked (in some ways) to its disadvantage as two new major roads have been laid across the area. Some types of employment have come to an end, but new companies and firms have moved in. Houses which once had servants have been divided into flats and sold, and changing property values have transformed whole estates of modest houses into 'exclusive' areas. Known in the 19th century for the food it sent to London (the Williams' pear was first grown near Turnham Green Terrace), in our time Chiswick is known for the Boat Race, shoe polish, Palladian architecture, battered wives and real ale!

However the process of recording and collecting the history of the area still goes on today, both at Gunnersbury Park Museum and at Chiswick Library. The collections of photographs, prints, books, diaries, local authority records and memories on tape have been created mainly by donations from local people. We hope that this book will make people more aware of the history of this area, and will in turn help to create the collections which will be used to tell the history of our time to the future.

James Wisdom
Chairman
The Brentford and Chiswick Local History Society

Church Street

1.   Church Street *c.*1905, looking towards the River Thames, with Sich's brewery store on the right. This street has many connections with the Sich family and their brewery. John Sich founded the Lamb brewery in 1773. It was situated behind the houses on the left-hand side of Church Street. The two public houses, which can be seen in the background, The Lamb Tap and The Burlington Arms were owned by the brewery until it was sold in 1923 to the Isleworth Brewery, which in turn was sold to Watney, Combe Reid & Company. The Lamb Tap ceased to be a public house about 1910, but The Burlington Arms continued until about 1923, when both buildings were converted into private homes. The Lamb Tap is an 18th-century building, but The Burlington Arms was originally 16th-century tenements.

The house on the extreme left, Wisteria Cottage, is 18th century, and was the home of Arthur Sich, a partner in the brewery. The building to its right was originally one house, also built in the 18th century and owned by the Sich family. In 1950 it was divided into two dwellings called Ferry House and Brampton House. On the right where the brewery store stood two modern houses were built about 1966 and 1973.

2.   St Nicholas, the old parish church of Chiswick by the river at the south end of Church Street, has been rebuilt and altered many times. The first recorded vicar was John Belemains or Belemus, who died in 1252. The picture shows the interior before the rebuilding in 1882–4. The galleries were built when new aisles of brick had been added on the south side in 1772 and on the north in 1817. The galleries and the old pews were removed in the 1882 rebuilding.

Chiswick Mall

3. Thornycroft's shipbuilding yard, the rebuilt St Nicholas Church, Chiswick Vicarage and Woodroffe House photographed from the river at the end of the last century.

   The Thornycroft boat-yard flourished from 1864 until the firm moved to Southampton in 1904. Two of their steam launches can be seen moored in front of the yard. Between the yard and St Nicholas Church are the low roofs of some of the cottages in Fisherman's Place, which were demolished in the 1930s. The 15th-century tower of the church stands above the 1882–4 rebuilding of the nave and chancel.

   The Old Vicarage was built in 1657 at a cost of £260, which was collected from the parishioners. The bow front was added in the 18th century and with the wooden railings in front of the vicarage is shown in an 1806 painting by John Varley. When this building was sold as a private house a new vicarage was built in 1973 in the grounds to the east.

4.   A turn-of-the-century photograph of the back of Bedford House, Chiswick Mall, also showing, on the left, part of Eynham House. A house on the site was built or remodelled by Edward Russell, son of the 4th Earl of Bedford, in the 17th century and may form part of the present buildings which, although altered and added to at various times, are now basically 18th century. After the death of Edward Russell the property was acquired by Thomas Plukenett, through the marriage of whose daughter it passed to the Woodroffe family, the owners until the 1920s.

For a time Bedford House was the home of Warwick Draper, a barrister and local historian. He was the author of *Chiswick,* published in 1923, a second edition of which was issued in 1973. Warwick Draper died tragically after a fall from the roof of Bedford House in May 1926. He was one of the founders of the Chiswick Residents' Committee, formed to oppose the establishment of gas works on Duke's Meadows. He was a member of the Labour Party, whose Parliamentary candidate he was to have been at Chiswick had he lived.

Later residents of Bedford House were Sir Arthur Ellis, physician, and Sir Michael Redgrave.

5.   The Red Lion public house photographed prior to its closure about 1914. Since 1916 the building has reverted to a private house. Built *c.*1700, it was a licensed premises by 1722. As it stands opposite the Draw Dock on Chiswick Mall it would have been much frequented by the men working on the barges and the carters transporting goods from the river craft.

The building contains the original staircase and one original fireplace. The front of the building has been refaced, and the attic storey is a later addition.

6.   A turn-of-the-century photograph of spritsail barges moored at Chiswick Mall. During the second half of the 19th century and the early years of this century these barges would have been a common sight along Chiswick Mall. The barge in the foreground was registered in Rochester, from where there was a trade in transporting both bricks and cement up river. The osiers on Chiswick Eyot can be seen on the right.

7.   The rear of College House photographed from the garden in 1854. This house, which was demolished in 1875, was situated on Chiswick Mall on the eastern corner of the junction with Chiswick Lane. It had been built in 1710, replacing the Prebendal Manor House, which was used from 1564 until the end of the 17th century by scholars from Westminster School during epidemics of the plague.

Agnes and Mary Berry lived here from 1763. These two sisters were friends of Horace Walpole, and became his literary executors. In 1816 Charles Whittingham, who owned Chiswick Press, moved his printing presses into the house. Although the company opened a London office in 1828, work for the press continued at Chiswick until 1852. In its latter years the house was used as a lecture hall, and just before its demolition in 1875 Ellen Terry played there in a comedy. The site is now occupied by Suffolk, Heron and Staithe Houses, as well as Thames Bank.

8.   A photograph of the Christmas celebrations in the Children's Ward of Chiswick Hospital in 1927. Mr Dan Mason endowed a hospital in Burlington Lane in 1911, which in 1912 moved to a new building adjoining Rothbury House on Chiswick Mall. The conversion of Rothbury House and the cost of the new building were paid for by Mr Mason. Mr Mason was founder and chairman of Chiswick Polish Company, now part of the Reckett & Colman group. From 1926 the hospital was also used for maternity cases, nurses' accommodation was built and Rothbury House became the administrative block. The hospital was rebuilt in 1936.

    Under the National Health Act of 1948, the hospital became a branch of West Middlesex Hospital, closing in 1975. During the past ten years there have been several proposals for the use of the building, including the sale of the site to raise money for the Area Health Authority. Work has just started to convert the building into an old people's home, due to open in Autumn 1986.

Chiswick Lane

9. Bradmore House stood on the east side of Chiswick Lane, opposite the junction with Mawson Lane, until its demolition in 1896. The house was built about 1730 on the west side of Homefield, possibly for a Revd M. Hutchinson.

From the mid-18th century until his death in 1786, Dr William Rose ran a school at the house. Dr Rose came from Aberdeen, and was a friend of Dr Johnson. One of Dr Rose's daughters married Revd Charles Burney, brother of Fanny Burney.

10. The Manor House Farm in Chiswick Lane was built for Sir Stephen Fox between 1691 and 1694. Fox was the Member of Parliament for Salisbury, and held the appointments of First Commissioner of Horse and Paymaster General, as well as being a friend of King Charles II. The house was described as being built in red brick with stone dressings, and with a lofty roof of greenish slate. It was surrounded by huge elms, and its gardens to the west had grass lawns, orchards, and a bowling alley. On Sir Stephen Fox's death in 1716 it was inherited by his son Stephen, 1st Earl of Ilchester, who sold it to a gentleman by the name of Welstead. In 1790 it was occupied by Dr Horne, who kept a school there.

By 1851 the Tuke family had purchased the house for a private lunatic asylum, moving in 1896 to the larger premises at Chiswick House. Manor House Farm was then demolished. This photograph was taken in 1875. Ashbourne, Balfern, Cornwall, Dorchester, and Eastbury Groves were built across the site in 1897.

11. Some of the members of Chiswick Adult Schools, Women's Branch, at their formation in 1906. The adult school movement started in this country in 1843, although the Chiswick Adult School did not open until 1905. For the first year it catered only for men, meeting on Sunday mornings from 8 a.m. until 10 a.m. at The Mission Hall, Fraser Street. The group was non sectarian although the central purpose was the free but reverent study of the bible.

The women's branch met at The Mission Hall on Monday evenings. In 1907 meetings moved to the Primitive Methodist School Room in Fisher's Lane. By 1908 they were considering purchasing premises of their own. The year 1910 saw them meeting in Kensington House in Turnham Green Terrace, but by 1916 they had moved to the Friends' Meeting House in Essex Place. No activities of the school can be traced after 1920.

Chiswick High Road

12. Nos. 62–68 Chiswick High Road, seen in 1930. No. 64 was occupied by Wakefields Limited, photographers, from 1908 until 1963. Wakefields were well known in Ealing (where they had a shop by 1890) and in Brentford and Chiswick. They were responsible for many photographs of the area taken early this century, some of which appear in this publication. On the left can be seen the West London Trades Hall and Institute, which opened in 1920. The Amalgamated Engineering Union leased the building until 1950 when they purchased it, but by 1959 it required such substantial sums of money to be spent on renovations that they proposed that it should be sold.

All the buildings appear on the Tithe Map of Chiswick 1847, and were possibly built c.1820–40. At the end of the last century they housed schools. Today both buildings remain; No. 64 known as Burlington House and No. 66 occupied by Chiswick Trades and Social Club.

13.   The inauguration of the London United Electric Tramways system, which took place on 10th July 1901. This photograph shows the guests outside the Chiswick Tram Depot. The managing director of the company, Mr J. Clifton Robinson is shown centre, front, with a cigar in his hand. On his left is Lord Rothschild, who officially started the trams. Other guests included the First Lord of the Treasury and the Leader of the House of Commons, the Rt. Hon. Arthur J. Balfour, M.P..

A nine-car procession of decorated trams containing the guests travelled from Shepherds Bush to Southall and back, and then to the depot at Chiswick, where they were received by the chairman of London United Electric Tramways, Mr George White, and members of the board. The largest tram shed had been converted into a banqueting hall with pits boarded over and the floor covered with red felt, while on the walls and overhead flags and flowers formed the decoration.

The London United Electric Tramways operated services from Shepherds Bush to Uxbridge, Hounslow and Hampton Court. Their headquarters were at Chiswick, where they built their own power house, seen on the extreme right. This building is at present being converted into homes and recording studios. Trams ceased to operate in this area in 1935.

14. These two cottages stood on the north side of Chiswick High Road, east of Bohemia House. They were demolished in 1901 when the houses in Ennismore Avenue were built. Originally called Bohemia Avenue, the residents disliked the name and had it changed in 1908. The cottage on the right was called Vine Cottage, and that on the left Alpha Cottage. Both cottages had had an 18th-century façade added to their 17th-century, or earlier, structure. The photograph was taken between 1888, when the cottage on the left was numbered 98, and their demolition in 1901. The site is at present vacant.

15. Looking east along Chiswick High Road from Chiswick Lane, seen right, *c.*1910. This was the site of a turnpike gate from about 1859, when the gate was moved from Hammersmith. The toll-house was sited in the middle of the road, with side gates across Chiswick Lane to prevent travellers avoiding the main gate. The next turnpike on the road was outside the Bell Inn at Hounslow. The Hounslow gate was demolished in 1872, and presumably the Chiswick gate went at the same time. In 1937 the toll-house was to be found in the garden of 39 Oxford Road.

   The building on the extreme left, situated on the corner of Upham Park Road, was Munt Brothers, pianoforte manufacturers, and is now the London Motor Caravans car showrooms. The parade to the east of Upham Park Road, built in 1905, contained in 1910: Lennard's Limited, boot company; Frederick Bull, fancy goods; L.L. Leeder, estate agent; and William Perring, house furnishers. Today the eastern corner of Upham Park Road is occupied by Studio 91, and Nos. 96 and 98, to its east, are at present vacant.

16.   The old Roebuck public house in 1890, prior to its demolition and replacement by the present building. This was one of the major coaching inns in Chiswick, with a licence dating back to 1761, and possibly earlier. As regular coaching routes from London to the West Country were established from the mid-18th century, numerous coaching inns opened along Chiswick High Road to provide a change of horses and refreshment for the passengers. Through the archway on the left can be seen a part of the extensive stabling. This building was the subject of a coaching print by James Pollard in 1825, which showed a four-in-hand private drag standing outside the inn. The present public house was built at the time Thornton Avenue was created in the early 1890s. The public house was altered in 1971, and recently changed its name to The Chiswick Eyot.

17.   No. 147 Chiswick High Road was an early 18th-century house called Thorncroft. It was situated next to The Pack Horse and Talbot public house and was demolished in 1965. Until recently Hammond's Organ Showrooms occupied the site. This photograph was taken c.1900, when the house was occupied by Gilbert French, a physician and surgeon, who owned the house until the early 1940s.

18.   Sulhamstead House was one of many fine 18th-century buildings to be found on both sides of the High Road. It stood between Devonshire and Annandale Roads and was demolished c.1880. The original house is to the left with an extension to the right. In its last years it was owned by Col. William Wylde, a Superintendent at the Foreign Office, who lived there with his wife, five children, butler, cook, lady's maid, upper housemaid, nursery maid, and scullery maid. Devonshire Road was originally called Chiswick Field Lane.

19. Chiswick High Road, immediately east of The Prince of Wales public house, photographed in the early 1920s when a street market existed on the pavement in front of the shops along that section of the road.

The market was established in 1919 by the Council's Food Control Committee when two sites were made available to stall-holders on Saturdays at a cost of one shilling per day. The second site was in front of the National School by Essex Place. In 1924 a covered market was proposed, but at first this was opposed by Kingston Corporation. Later the plan was approved after an assurance was given to Kingston that it would not include a cattle market. The covered market was built at Camden House, 209 High Road.

Nos. 171–175 High Road was a terrace of shops built in 1905. At No. 171, on the left, was Arthur B. Braley, picture framer and dealer, who moved from Lawn Terrace, the buildings which previously occupied the site. Mr Braley was in business from 1888 until 1933. Mr Edgar Howard Barnes, a leather seller, occupied No. 173 from 1905, with the family only vacating the site in 1967.

On the extreme right can be seen the edge of the original Prince of Wales, licensed by 1826 and rebuilt c.1930. It closed in 1961 and was converted into flats with a shop on the ground floor.

20. The purpose built enclosed Market shortly after its opening in 1925. It contained forty-seven stalls but was not a success and by 1935 the number of stall-holders had dwindled to sixteen. The Brentford and Chiswick Borough Council closed it and converted the building together with the adjacent late 19th-century rebuilding of Linden House into a new fire station. The fire station moved to its present building in 1957, and the site is now occupied by Chiswick Police Station, which opened in 1972.

21. Camden House, Chiswick High Road, photographed in the mid-1890s shortly after it became the premises of the Chiswick Radical Club, who occupied the house for ten years from c.1893 - 1903. From about 1888 until 1893 the house was used by the Chiswick Conservative Club. The Goldhawk Building Society also had an office there from 1888 until 1896.

   The house was possibly built in the 18th century and was used as a girls' boarding school from about 1820 until 1871, when it changed to a boys' boarding school for a few years. From 1903 until 1908 the building was occupied by the British Moelline Company Limited; it was then left empty for a number of years until being used for the site of the Chiswick covered market in the 1920s.

   The adjoining premises, No. 10 Camden Terrace, were occupied by W.G. Tobutt, a furniture dealer from about 1893 until 1903. From his advertisement he also functioned as a furniture remover.

22. Linden House stood in the High Road until 1878, and was situated between the present entrances to Linden Gardens. It was an 18th-century house, lived in from c.1760 by Ralph Griffiths, a Staffordshire man who set up in London as a bookseller and publisher, producing the first literary review in England called *The Monthly Review*. Among Griffith's friends were Josiah Wedgwood and his partner Thomas Bentley, who also lived in Turnham Green.

   Griffith's grandson, Thomas Griffiths Wainewright, lived in the house after his grandfather's death in 1803. Wainewright was an artist, and his friends included Charles Lamb, Thomas Hood, Sir Thomas Lawrence and Flaxman, who were all entertained at the house. In London Wainewright posed as a dandy and became a poisoner, using a ring which contained poison in the form of crystals. He poisoned his uncle Thomas Griffiths, his mother-in-law Mrs Abercrombie, and her daughter Helen.

   Wainewright was arrested in 1837 for a forgery concerning an annuity, which was part of his wife's marriage settlement. He was imprisoned in Newgate prison until his trial, when he was found guilty and transported to Tasmania. He died there of apoplexy in 1847.

23. The Chiswick Special Constabulary photographed outside Chiswick Police Station at 208 Chiswick High Road, by the junction with Windmill Road, in November 1914. On the 11th November of that year they lined the Mall on the route that King George V and Queen Mary took to the State Opening of Parliament. The constabulary were under the command of Chief Sub-Inspector Gentry, possibly the gentleman wearing glasses, in the centre of the front row. The special constabulary undertook police duties in their spare time, to aid the police force depleted through men joining the services to serve in the First World War.

Chiswick was included within the Metropolitan Police Area from 1829, with the first police station being on the High Road, west of the Windmill public house. In 1874 a police station opened on the east corner of Windmill Road, to be replaced in 1972 by the present police station by Linden Gardens.

Back Common

24. These old wooden cottages on Back Common Row were photographed in 1896. They were demolished early this century and replaced in 1907 by Victor Villas, which are situated in Back Common Road, by the turning for Windmill Road.

25. No. 12 Jessop's Row stood at the end of the row facing the High Road, behind Goodban's shop. It was demolished about 1951 having been there from the beginning of the 18th century or earlier, when it was a small inn called The Follies. By the mid-19th century it was occupied by the Gould family, who were market gardeners. Mrs Elizabeth Gould, who can be seen in this photograph of *c.*1890, was left a widow by 1871, and ran a laundry from the house until early this century. Jessop's Row later became Jessop's Road, and was situated off Belmont Road.

Bedford Park

26.   A photograph of the original 1877 poster, by Maurice B. Adams, to advertise the proposed first Garden Suburb in England, which became Bedford Park. The poster executed in collaboration with Norman Shaw shows, from the right, three designs by Norman Shaw. The house on the extreme left was designed by E.W. Goodwin, F.S.A.

Bedford Park was planned by Jonathan T. Carr, a cloth merchant, who purchased 24 acres of land surrounding three Georgian houses. E.W. Goodwin designed the first houses in 1875, followed by Norman Shaw in 1877. By 1883, 490 houses had been built on 113 acres. The roads were planned to preserve mature trees on the site and to resemble a village. Road names were chosen after personalities and events from Queen Anne's reign.

In 1881 financial backing was provided by a company called Bedford Park Limited, which collapsed in 1886. Bedford Park Estate Limited acquired part of the assets and completed unfinished roads. The first residents were a mixture of middle-class Londoners and people from the arts such as J.B. Yeats, William Terriss, and Pinero.

Chiswick High Road

27. Chiswick High Road looking east from the junction with Linden Gardens, seen right, in the early years of this century. The shops on the north side of the road from the left were: Marsh, a corn dealer; H.E. Veal, watch maker and jeweller, who was there until *c.*1920; and next to him Home & Colonial, grocer. W.H. Dadd's shoe shop in 1910 moved to the western side of the corn dealer.

This photograph shows that by early this century the High Road had become a shopping street, and that most of the private houses had disappeared. Today the following shops occupy the buildings on the left: Nos. 260–262, Home Charm Wallpaper; and Nos. 256–258, Lipton's grocer.

28. Myrtle Cottage was situated on the High Road, three doors west of Fisher's Lane. The premises were occupied by Henry Eydmann, carpenter and builder, from *c.*1855 until *c.*1880, when Mr Eydmann died. At that time the building was demolished and the present terrace of buildings between Fisher's Lane and Holly Road was constructed. The Eydmann family played a prominent part in the affairs of Chiswick during the second half of the 19th century as surveyors, builders, firemen and shopkeepers, and are mentioned several times in this publication.

29. Chiswick High Road *c*.1914, showing left, Goodban's Department Store, with its arcades at Nos. 326–332. This was formerly William Stone's store and was acquired by Mr Percy Goodban in 1909. In 1928 Goodbans was sold to Mr Cecil J. Cooper, who retained the name. On his death in 1962 at the age of 92 years, he was succeeded by his son, Mr John Cooper. The store closed on 13th February 1974, when Mr John Cooper retired, and the premises were sold. Boots and Catos stores now occupy the site.
On the right-hand side of the road at Nos. 257–9, the old Chiswick Post Office is marked by an illuminated lamp. The Post Office moved to a new building in Heathfield Terrace on 4th July 1966, and the old building is now a branch of The Trustee Savings Bank.

30. The High Road in 1925, showing the Turnham Green National School buildings on the left. The school opened in 1848, built on wasteland, and financed by a parliamentary grant. It was maintained from subscriptions, collections from special sermons, and by children paying a few pence a week to attend. By 1867 the boys' and infants' departments were occupying this site, with the girls' department acquiring a new building in Horticultural Place. The boys moved out in 1897, followed by the infants in 1905 when Belmont Road School opened.

No. 376 High Road, on the right, was a new building in 1925, occupied by F.D. Allwright who opened a car hire firm, which later became a car accessory shop owned by the same family until 1985. Next door was W. Whiteside, fishmonger, whose shop in 1926 became the property of R. Portch; his family still run the fishmonger's shop on the site. The school buildings survived until after the Second World War, but are now the site of Kall Kwik Print; Reed's employment agency; and the Argos Discount Store.

31.   This is the oldest known photograph of Turnham Green, taken from the Green on the evening of 16th August 1863, showing the buildings on the High Road either side of Caroline Place, which can be seen to the west of The Crown and Anchor public house. This building was not listed as an inn in 1826, but was by the mid-1830s, and was altered and extended *c.*1887. Erected between 1851 and 1861, the low building in the centre of Caroline Place was a smithy, then owned by John Tutt, which survived in business until about 1917. In 1925 Frank Allwright's motor accessory shop was built on part of the site. Wellington Place was the name of the terrace to the right, built *c.*1820-40, and partly replaced in 1887 by the present buildings. Today about five shops remain, having been built over the gardens of a portion of the terrace.

On the left, the building, of *c.*1840, by Caroline Place was a beerhouse known

for many years as The Ship at Anchor. In the 1851 census it was called The Chaffcutter's Arms. It closed about 1908, and the premises became a fruiterer's shop. It is now the site of Portch's fishmonger's shop. The hand pump on the edge of Turnham Green produced water which was used for many purposes, including laying the dust on the road during the summer. The pond on the right-hand side had been filled in by 1865.

The long shadow, visible across the Green and produced by the evening sun, is the spire of Christchurch. The railings along the High Road were then newly erected and the trees newly planted. The marks on the photograph are there because the original glass plate negative has been damaged. The High Road would have been a busy bustling place, but because of the long exposure required for the photograph all the moving images have disappeared.

32.   This photograph was taken in 1910, prior to the demolition of these buildings for the erection of the Chiswick Empire, which opened in 1912 and closed in 1959. At the same time the Old Pack Horse public house was rebuilt, and the scaffolding on the extreme left could be part of that operation. Bissley's printing works, there since 1894, received new premises. The Bricklayers Arms beerhouse closed and was not rebuilt. The premises had been a beerhouse from at least the mid-19th century. Smith, the boot maker, and extreme left, Barratt, the undertaker, occupied their premises in 1887, but in 1851 Barratt had been a carpenter, and a harness maker had occupied the boot maker's shop. The shop on the right-hand corner was a newsagents' from 1894, and before that a corn stores. Today, the sites on the High Road are occupied by, from the left, Nos. 424, Top Hat Cleaners; 422, Granada Television Rental; 418, Chiswick Gallery; 416, Holland & Barrett's health food shop; and 414, the entrance to the IBM office block.

33.   Trams in Chiswick High Road showing, on the right, the railings around Turnham Green which were placed there in 1861 in imitation of Kew Green. The photograph was taken by The Photographic Tourist Association, who occupied 4 Heathfield Terrace from 1899 until 1908.

   The shop on the left, with a blind over its side window, was No. 402, The National Telephone Company Limited's public call office. The advertisement in front of the shop advertises a parcel service to London. To its right was the Royal Standard Laundry, whose window contained an advertisement for an ironer. Next door was William Monk's confectioner's shop, which today is the western end of Waitrose's supermarket. No. 402 High Road is at present occupied by Reed's employment agency.

34.   The Old Pack Horse on the corner of Acton Lane was originally built in 1643 and has one of the oldest licences in Chiswick. It stood opposite Turnham Green when it was a place frequented by highwaymen and footpads. The present building was erected in 1911.

In 1696 there was a plot to assassinate King William III as he travelled along Wellesley Road, then called Turnham Green Lane, on his return to Kensington Palace after hunting in Richmond Park. The conspirators plotted his assassination in both The Old Pack Horse and The Bohemia Head inns. The plot was leaked, the King put off his hunting, and many of the conspirators were caught. In 1725 when Jonathon Wild, the highwayman, was on trial, he called as his witness Hays of The Pack Horse on Turnham Green. Horace Walpole baited his horses there when travelling from Twickenham to London.

King George III, Queen Charlotte, and the Princesses Elizabeth, Augusta, Mary, Sophia, and Amelia in 1808 were travelling from London to Windsor, when on crossing Turnham Green, one of the leading horses and postillion fell. A second postillion saved the King's coach from overturning. The King on alighting from his coach found himself walking through mud of a great depth. He had to wait the arrival of the Queen's carriage to be able to continue his journey. The injured postillion was taken to The Pack Horse Inn and put to bed. This photograph was taken c.1900.

35.   Acton Green Road, now Acton Lane, *c*.1897, seen from the junction with Chiswick High Road. The grocer's shop on the left was newly built in 1897 for Gapps Ltd., who occupied the site until 1930. D. Blackwell, rag and bottle merchant, only occupied the site for two years at the end of the last century, prior to the demolition of that terrace of buildings, and the renaming of that stretch of road Acton Lane. The tall building on the right was Pope & Sons, West London depository, demolished *c*.1971, and beyond can be seen Lorne Villas and Ivy Cottages. The address of these three buildings was always Acton Lane, and they were sited where one of the entrances now leads to Sainsbury's Supermarket in Essex Place. The site of Gapp's grocery shop is now occupied by Hooper & Cox, bookmakers.

Turnham Green

36. Heathfield Terrace in 1934 looking west from the Army & Navy Stores Depository, just prior to the demolition of Nos. 3–9 Heathfield Terrace. The depository was built in 1871 on the site of one of three blocks of buildings built for the 3rd West Middlesex Militia, possibly at the time of the Crimea War. The site is now awaiting redevelopment. The houses next to the depository were replaced by Heathfield Court flats in 1936. On the extreme right is one of the Turnham Green National School Buildings demolished c.1972.

37. Cricket at Turnham Green during summer weekends has been a common sight back into the last century. This photograph of about 1912 shows, on the extreme left, two early motor buses. The land to the north of Christchurch was proposed as a site for a parish hall in 1911. This led to a great controversy as to whether Turnham Green should be built upon. It was resolved in 1913 by an exchange of lands with Chiswick Urban District Council, and the parish hall was built at the junction of Heathfield Terrace and Gardens, on the site of Sutton Lodge.

38. Turnham Green from Chiswick High Road, seen early this century, showing Christchurch, designed by Sir Charles Gilbert Scott in 1843, at a cost of £8,500. On the extreme left can be seen the Army & Navy Depository, with to the right, Chiswick Town Hall built in 1901, to a design by the council surveyor, A. Ramsden. From 1874 until 1901 Chiswick Vestry Hall had stood on the site. The houses in Heathfield Terrace, on either side of the Town Hall, cannot be dated more precisely than the early 19th century, and are all grade II listed buildings.

39. The ceremony on Turnham Green on Tuesday, 18th October 1932 at which the Charter of Incorporation for the creation of the Borough of Brentford and Chiswick was handed to the Charter Mayor, Mr James Clements, J.P., seen centre right, by the Lord Lieutenant of Middlesex, Lord Rochdale, centre left, on behalf of King George V. The Charter Mayoress, Mrs J. Clements is seen to the right of the High Sheriff of Middlesex, Lt. Col. M.F.M.S. Kittoe. On the extreme right is the Deputy Charter Mayor, Councillor F.S. Hayburn.

The day commenced with the Mayoral procession greeting the King's representative and the county dignitories at Kew Bridge. The procession then made its way to Turnham Green for the ceremony, followed by luncheon in the Town Hall. In the afternoon a long procession of decorated lorries and carts, and a carriage containing the Mayor and Mayoress processed around the borough, finishing in Boston Manor Park. The day ended at Duke's Meadow with community singing and a stupendous firework display.

Chiswick first joined with Brentford in 1927 as an Urban District. Chiswick had been an Urban District from 1896, and prior to that had been administered by Chiswick Local Board from 1875.

Chiswick High Road

40.   The Robin Hood and Little John beerhouse, just prior to its demolition in 1896. It was situated four doors west of the junction with Acton Green Road (now called Acton Lane). The present public house was built in 1897 on the adjacent site, to the west of the building in the photograph. The beerhouse cottage dated back to at least the 18th century, but the first reference to a beerhouse called The Robin Hood and Little John appears in the rate book of 1869. In 1851 the premises were occupied by a corn and coal merchant.

41.   The Grange was built on orchard ground near Gunnersbury Station *c.*1874, by and for William J. Trahearne, who was Chiswick Local Board's Surveyor. In 1889 it was sold to a builder called Kendall, who lived in The Grange while he developed Grange Road in the 1890s. The house was demolished in the late 1930s and a block of flats with the same name was completed in 1939.

42.   Gunnersbury Lane, now called Gunnersbury Avenue, seen from the junction with Chiswick High Road early this century. This junction formed one of the boundaries between Chiswick, Brentford and Acton. Looking north, on the left, can be seen buildings belonging to Gunnersbury Cottage. At the end of the last century this was a market garden run by Thomas Jefferys. The cottage survived until Gunnersbury Lane was widened in the late 1920s; the name changed to Gunnersbury Avenue in 1931. Some outbuildings of the market garden survive, but are at present threatened with demolition.

The orchard on the right was not built upon until 1933, when Elkington Carriage Company Limited, coach builders, opened there, becoming Elkington Motors. Today the premises are still a garage, owned by Warwick Wright Motors Limited.

43.   This house was at various times known as Stile Hall or Sydney House, and was situated west of Wellesley Road at its junction with Chiswick High Road. A previous house on the site was leased by Johann Zoffany, the artist, from 1769 to 1772. Luke Wetton purchased that house in 1789 and replaced it by the house in the photograph, minus the top two storeys. The Wetton family were known to Zoffany, as there is a painting by him entitled *Mr. and Mrs. Peter Wetton of London Style House, Chiswick.*

In 1880 ownership passed from John Wetton to the Rt. Hon. R.R. Bignell, who added the top two storeys. This photograph was taken in 1890 when the house was sold to Harvey Smith, who in 1891 demolished it and in 1892 had the houses in Stile Hall Gardens built. Stile Hall was at times known as Sydney House because it was sited close to a 16th-century house lived in by Lady Mary Sidney, mother of Sir Philip Sidney. This lady retired to Chiswick after nursing Queen Elizabeth I through an attack of smallpox.

A house on the east side of Wellesley Road by the junction with Chiswick High Road called London Style House was built about 1660 for the Hammett family, who lived there until it was demolished in 1869. London Style was a name used for the section of the main road from Kew Bridge to Gunnersbury Lane. London Style Farm was situated where Brentford Market was built at the end of the 19th century. The use of the name London Style for both the area and various buildings in the locality has led to considerable confusion over the ownership of individual houses.

Strand on the Green

44.   A photograph taken at the end of the 19th century showing the second Kew Bridge, built in 1789 and replaced by the present bridge in 1903. The three buildings on the right were used by Simon Camille's French Steam Laundry & Cleaning Works, established in 1860. In 1905 the purpose built Pier House Laundry building was erected for the firm on the opposite side of the road. This closed in 1973. The buildings in the photograph were demolished in the late 1920s and the site landscaped to form a riverside promenade.

The central building was said to have been a public house prior to 1860. The steam crane by the bridge was probably used by the laundry for unloading the coal used to power its machinery. The cross poles over the doorway on the right, also operated as a primitive crane.

45.   This photograph of Strand on the Green taken from Oliver Island can be dated to pre-1907 as in that year The Bell and Crown public house, which can be seen behind the trees on the left, was rebuilt.

The houses to the right of the inn survive, and from the left are No. 71, with the central bay which was built at the end of the 18th century and No. 70, which was refronted in the 19th century. Nos. 68 and 69, known as Carlton House, were built at the beginning of the 18th century, as were the adjoining pair. The house on the right was built c.1704. It was purchased in 1790 by the artist Johann Zoffany, who lived there until his death.

46. · An early 20th-century photograph of Strand on the Green, with the Ship Inn seen on the extreme left. This inn was licensed by 1722 and closed in 1910, when it was converted into a private house. Adjoining the Ship can be seen an early 19th-century terrace of houses, numbered 52 to 55, and further east two malthouses whose square roofs can still be seen on the skyline.

Malthouses were operating here from at least the late 17th century, malting barley for the London market. They were situated by the river to make it easy to import the barley and coal, and to export the finished malt. These buildings are 19th century. The operation of the malthouse can be seen, as the maltster has varied the position of the shutters in the window openings to allow air to circulate differently on each floor, where the barley would be at different stages of germination. Numbered 47, the premises are now used as offices.

47. The River Thames at Strand on the Green looking towards Kew Bridge in the early years of this century. The three spritsail barges and their accompanying lighters belonged to Charles Murrell, a barge builder, who occupied the premises immediately west of The City Barge Inn from 1902 until 1927.

Strand on the Green grew up as a fishing community in the 17th century with larger houses being built in the 18th century, which attracted residents such as Johann Zoffany, the artist. The barge and lighter trade expanded in the 19th century, as it did at Chiswick Mall and even more so in Brentford.

On the left is Oliver Island formed over many centuries. Buildings were erected on the island after 1777 by the City of London Navigation Committee and transferred in 1857 to the Thames Conservancy Board. In this photograph a boat building and repair business can be seen on the island. In 1979 the Port of London Authority, who had owned the island since 1911, leased it to the London Natural History Society.

48. The City Barge, which was licensed by 1786. Sometime between then and 1807 it changed its name from The Maypole Inn, in honour of the City of London state barge called *The Maria Wood,* which was kept in the reach, with her barge house opposite on the Surrey bank.

A land mine in 1940 destroyed most of the inn, and the pair of Elizabethan cottages to the right. Today all that remains of the 18th-century building is the Old Bar below the level of the footpath. The barge with the block and tackle, in the foreground, had a mast which could be lowered for travelling under the bridges.

49. The Bull's Head *c.*1905, looking east. The building was licensed by 1722, and was one of several riverside inns which played an important part in the life of this riverside community. An inn was a place where cargoes and crews were arranged, money, goods and messages left and collected. They were essential places for the boatmen who moved up and down the river. The projecting brickwork, in the right foreground, is a set of stairs, which gave access to the river from the public house.

Grove Park

50. Grove Park Road looking towards Strand on the Green, seen from the junction with Grove Park Terrace at the turn of the century. The garden in the foreground belonged to Isis House, built c.1876 and converted into flats, known as Isis Court, in 1927. The entrance gate opposite led to a market garden run by Mr William Mills. Houses were built on this site early this century.

The buildings on the south side of Grove Park Road are, from the right, the Devonshire Boat House, opened in 1871 by the Lambeth boat builder called Frank Maynard which is now owned by the firm Bason & Arnold, and two gothic houses designed in the early 1870s by William Sergeant, an architect, who lived in Grove Park.

51. The level crossing in Grove Park Terrace looking towards Grove Park Road c.1910.

The London and South Western Railway loop line from Barnes to Hounslow was constructed in 1849. A foot-bridge was built alongside the crossing in 1868 and, possibly at the same time, the single gate was erected. This was opened manually by the gatekeeper and there were numerous complaints from residents about the long delays in opening the gate.

In 1901 the horse omnibus from Grove Park to Turnham Green was hit on the crossing by a light engine travelling towards London. The two horses and one man, who was helping to water the horses for the day, were killed. Fortunately there were no passengers in the bus at the time, but the driver and conductor were seriously injured. The single gate was not replaced by double gates until about 1913–14, and the modern continental barrier was installed in 1973.

The area around Grove Park was developed from 1860 onwards.

52. This lake in Grove House grounds, photographed about 1901, can be traced back to the mid-18th century, and is now the site of Chiswick Quay Marina. The lake was used for punting, and contained an island in the centre with a grotto at its eastern end.

During the First World War a canal and lock were constructed and the lake converted into a barge yard for the firm Holland Hammer & Cubitts, who made concrete barges which carried ammunition to France. An adjacent gravel pit provided gravel for the concrete. About 1920 the first houseboats arrived and in 1932 it became Cubitts Yacht Basin. The gravel pit was filled in with waste, and the surface allowed to settle for tennis courts. Later caravans occupied the site, and in 1958 Thames Village was built, the maisonettes each being built on a raft of concrete.

53. Established as a yacht basin from 1920, Cubitts Basin provided moorings for about fifty boats. Some people lived there all year, but others only used it for winter moorings. In 1936 it was purchased by a company who proposed to develop the site, and in 1939 notice was given to the Cubitts Yacht Basin Company to vacate. The Second World War prevented this development commencing. Caravans were allowed on the adjacent site until given notice to quit in 1952 for the proposed Thames Village development, completed in 1958.

In 1965 a proposal to build a block of forty flats and eighty-four houses and to fill in the basin was opposed by both boat owners and local residents and was rejected after a public enquiry. A second proposal for five blocks of three-storey maisonettes and keeping the yacht basin was passed by Hounslow Council in 1967, but a later proposal led to a second public enquiry.

The boat owners were given notice to quit in 1968, and although they put their case to the Ombudsman and to the High Court they had to leave in September 1969. In 1968 permission was given for twenty-eight houses and thirty maisonettes to be built, with a smaller and deeper non-residential basin, clubhouse and auxilliary facilities. This proposal did not go ahead and in 1970 two further plans were put forward. The second for sixty-eight houses was granted provided the riverside land was landscaped with a riverside walk. The developer was to rebuild the basin with a clubhouse, harbour office, chandlery and boat house.

Preparatory work in filling in the basin commenced in 1971, but when detailed plans were submitted to Hounslow Council they were refused. In 1972 the basin was strengthened and decreased in size and new plans for houses were accepted by both Hounslow Council and The Royal Fine Arts Commission. The first houses were completed in 1974, but only half had been sold in 1976. Chiswick Quay was the name of the site, with the basin being known as Chiswick Quay Marina, but it is little used as it is almost impossible to get in or out, other than at high tide.

54. Bathers in Chiswick Open Air Swimming Baths in Edensor Road on a summer Sunday morning about 1927. The land for the baths was purchased from His Grace the Duke of Devonshire in 1905 for £650. For several years Chiswick Urban District Council debated whether money should be spent on building the baths. In 1908 it was decided that they should be built at a cost of not more than £1,750, and they opened in 1910 having cost £1,650. Separate sessions were held for men and boys and women and girls. At weekends there were special family sessions. School children also had their own sessions. In 1920 an article appeared in *The Chiswick Times* about the bohemian atmosphere at weekends when 'mixed bathing' was allowed. The baths were closed after the 1980 summer season, which caused many protests.

55. Chiswick County School for Girls opened in Burlington Lane in 1916. This photograph was taken at the prize giving in 1926. Mrs M.E. Tuke, J.P., seen left wearing a hat, presided over the proceedings and Miss Sparks, centre, from St Hugh's College, Oxford University, presented the prizes. Miss G. Hedley, on the right, was the headmistress from the school's opening until her retirement in 1936.

On the adjacent site in 1926 Chiswick County School for Boys opened. The two schools joined to become a coeducational grammar school in 1966, and in 1968 became Chiswick Comprehensive School on its amalgamation with Staveley Road School.

Burlington Lane

56.   The south front of Chiswick House *c.*1930, showing the two wings added in 1788 to a design by James Wyatt, for Georgiana, 5th Duchess of Devonshire. Chiswick House was designed in 1727 by Richard Boyle, 3rd Earl of Burlington, assisted by Colen Campbell, and completed in 1736 after Campbell's death. William Kent was then employed to complete the interior design. On completion the villa was meant to be the most perfect example of Palladian architecture in England.

In 1753 the estate was inherited by the Marquis of Hartington, later the 4th Duke of Devonshire, through his marriage to the Earl of Burlington's daughter. In 1928 the 9th Duke of Devonshire put the estate up for sale, and only its purchase by Middlesex County Council prevented it being sold for development.

The County Council leased the property and grounds to Brentford and Chiswick Urban District Council for use as a public park. During the Second World War the house was transferred by Deed of Gift to the Ministry of Works (now the Department of the Environment). The two Wyatt wings were demolished and the villa restored to its original splendour, opening to the public in 1958. In 1965 the London Borough of Hounslow became the owners of the grounds, and in 1983 English Heritage became responsible for the management of the house.

57.   Burlington Lane in 1903 looking towards the south west, with the boundary wall to Chiswick House just visible on the right. The hedge on the left has been replaced by the houses between Corney and Grantham Roads. Originally called 'The Crescent', these houses were built in 1907. Burlington Lane used to run one hundred yards closer to the south front of the Palladian Villa, but in 1828 the Duke of Devonshire obtained an Act of Parliament to move a length of the public road southwards, to avoid the public gazing on the house.

58. The garden side of Boston House in Chiswick Square photographed early this century. The three-storey building on the left is the original house built in the 1680s, which was extended and refronted by Viscount Boston in 1740. There were later additions to the building in the 19th century. It became a school for young ladies in the early 19th century, run by Mrs Nethercliff. In the 1880s it was known as Boston House College, but by 1893 it was occupied by a Roman Catholic Sisterhood and known as St Veronica's Retreat, changing to Nazareth House from 1913–20. From 1922 it was a club for the female employees of Chiswick Products Limited. In the early 1980s the house was divided into four dwellings, with five neo-Georgian houses being built in the grounds.

59. Devonshire Road looking towards its junction with Burlington Lane, opposite The George and Devonshire public house, photographed about 1912.

The George and Devonshire is a late 17th-century building with an 18th-century refronting. This building and two cottages were purchased in 1700 by Thomas Mawson for £70. The inn at that time was called The George. Thomas Mawson also purchased the Bedford House brewhouse in 1701 and this, with other buildings on the adjacent site, became the Fuller Smith & Turner brewery. The gateway to the left of The George and Devonshire advertises C.W. Payne, removal contractors, who was also a greengrocer and fruiterer, operating from Chiswick Lane. After 1917 both operations centred on Chiswick Lane.

Thomas Nichols was a builder at Vine House, Church Street, from at least 1887. He was responsible for building some of the houses in Airedale Avenue c.1902. He was succeeded by William Nichols, who in about 1912 started as an undertaker and monumental mason, in Mawson Lane, as well as continuing the building business in Church Street. The building firm continued in business until 1952, and is now the premises of R. Ball & Company, builder. The three-storey single cell house on the corner of Burlington Lane and Devonshire Road was a 16th-century building demolished in the early 1930s for the widening of Burlington Lane. This end of Devonshire Road was altered in the late 1950s for the construction of the Hogarth roundabout.

Hogarth Lane

60.   Hogarth House in the late 19th century photographed by one of Taunt's photographers. William Hogarth, the artist, lived in this early 18th-century house from 1749 until the night before his death in 1764. The house would then have been in the heart of the country, and would have provided the artist with a country retreat from his town house in Leicester Fields. After his death his wife lived there until her death in 1789, when the house became the property of her cousin Mary Lewis. Later it was the home of the Revd Henry Francis Cary, Curate of Chiswick. By 1874 it had fallen into decay. In 1891 it was purchased by Alfred Dawson, but was up for sale again in 1900. Local people failed to raise enough money to buy the house and so Lieutenant-Colonel Robert Shipway of Grove House purchased and restored the house, opening it to the public in 1902. In 1909 he conveyed it to Middlesex County Council for use as a Hogarth Museum. Ownership passed in 1965 to the London Borough of Hounslow.

   The tree in the photograph is a mulberry tree, which still produces mulberries each year. It bore fruit in Hogarth's day, although it was once struck by lightning. Hogarth braced and girded it with chains and stanchions and it continued to give fruit. During the Second World War, bombs falling in the area caused the tree to be uprooted and the hollow trunk split in two and broke. However, experts from Kew Gardens were able to coax it back to life.

61.   The north entrance to the Chiswick House estate photographed before 1897. The gates, which were situated opposite the south end of Duke's Avenue, have an interesting history.

   Originally they stood at the entrance to Heathfield House, which was on the south west side of Turnham Green. When this 18th-century house was demolished in 1837, the gates were purchased by the Duke of Devonshire and placed at the north entrance to Chiswick House. In 1897 they were moved to Devonshire House in Piccadilly.

   Early this century they were bought for the Nation from the Queen Victoria Memorial Fund, and in 1921 were erected at the entrance to Green Park in Piccadilly.

Duke's Avenue

62. The view in Duke's Avenue looking north into Chiswick High Road in the early years of the century. Chiswick Public Library, seen left, was prior to 1897 the home of the Sanderson family, owners of the famous wallpaper factory. The wall on the extreme left surrounded Devonhurst, a large house built in 1873 for Edmund Watts, a ship owner, and demolished about 1900.

In the distance on the left is the Roman Catholic Church of Our Lady of Grace, built in 1886 after the demolition of an earlier church built in 1864 and called St Mary's Church. The Earl of Bute, then living in Chiswick House, contributed towards the cost of the present church. By 1903 its name had changed to Our Lady of Grace and St Edward. The campanile was added in 1932, to a design by Sir Giles Gilbert Scott, architect of Liverpool Anglican Cathedral. It was a memorial to Chiswick Catholics killed in the First World War.

The shops which can be seen in the High Road show, from the left, Arthur Dempsey, draper and milliner; and Arthur Kemble Kemp, grocer. The houses on the right-hand side of Duke's Avenue were built from 1886 onwards. The exit from Bourne Place into Duke's Avenue did not appear until 1911.

63. North Lodge, built c.1888, stood on the corner of Bourne Place and Duke's Avenue, and was lived in at the turn of the century by Henry Eydmann, a local builder. Born in 1858 he followed his father into the building trade. He was an apprentice in London, and from 1852 onwards was in business at Chiswick. In 1859 he was appointed rate collector for Chiswick at £35 per year, resigning a few years after the Chiswick Improvement Commissioners came into being. With the formation of Chiswick Urban District Council, in 1894 he was elected councillor for the Turnham Green Ward. In business he was responsible for repairs and decorations to Chiswick House. He was also one of the first builders to work on the estate around Gunnersbury Station.

Later the house was lived in by Mr Sydney Eydmann, possibly his son, who was assistant surveyor to Chiswick Urban District Council. This photograph was taken in 1925 after ownership had passed out of the Eydmann family. From about 1958 until 1968 the property became the depot for Express Dairies. The house was then demolished and in the early 1980s the Roman Catholic Parish Centre was built on the site.

In Bourne Place can be seen the Chiswick Memorial Club, opened in 1919. Previously called Afton House, and before that Falkland House, this 18th-century building had been derelict for many years. It was given by Mr D. Mason for Chiswick Servicemen who had fought in the First World War.

64.   Sanderson's original wallpaper factory in Barley Mow Passage photographed *c.*1901. Arthur Sanderson set up an agency in 1860, moving to premises in Berners Street in London's West End in 1865. In 1879 he purchased this site in Chiswick, which had formerly been a part of the Militia Barracks. On the barrack square he had two buildings erected containing block tables and two roller printing machines. By 1896 he was employing about 250 people, and the premises covered almost an acre of ground. In 1899 the Chiswick branch became part of the Wallpaper Manufacturers Limited combine. C.F.A. Voysey designed a new building, which was completed by 1904 on the opposite side of the road. This building, which survives today, was the only factory building he designed. It housed the block and roller cutting departments, the hand grounding and leather sections, and the stencilling department on the top floor. Production continued at Chiswick until October 1928 when a fire destroyed nearly all the buildings on the south side of Barley Mow Passage. Within three months temporary floors had been erected and production recommenced at Chiswick. A site was chosen at Perivale, and a new factory was built there in 1929 and 1930. Production then moved from Chiswick to Perivale. The site was cleared and in 1936 the Devonshire Works and the building now known as the Barley Mow Workspace were built.

65.   The scene at the rear of Chiswick Library on 11th October 1928 after the Sanderson Wallpaper factory had been destroyed in a fire that also severely damaged a part of the library.

The fire started whilst most of the employees had gone to lunch, and was discovered by one man who remained at work. He smelt burning and discovered the fire in a room in the warehouse. He raised the alarm and Chiswick Fire Brigade was called. At first it looked as though the fire could be contained, but this proved impossible as firemen were unable to discover the seat of the fire, and were driven back by the acrid fumes. One hour after the fire commenced the roof nearest to the Army & Navy Depository caved in. Twelve fire-engines from London County Council had now arrived, and traffic was stopped in the High Road so that hoses could be run from the hydrants on the north side.

By early afternoon the library was in danger and a human chain was formed to remove books from the building. The area then had to be evacuated as the east wall of the factory collapsed. By 8 p.m. the library building was safe from further damage, but the fire still raged at the bottom of the factory. Eventually seventeen fire-engines and over a hundred firemen worked through the night until 4 a.m. to bring the fire under control.

As an aftermath of the fire Sanderson's built a new factory at Perivale, and the library building was repaired and altered, and a new wing was built. The library reopened in March 1931.

Little Sutton

66.   Sutton Court photographed *c.*1896, shortly before its demolition. In 1905 Sutton Court flats were built on the site. This house was possibly the third to be built here, and had been erected in 1790 for one Thomas King. Tenants in the early 19th century were Lt. Col. Henry Cavendish in the 1820s and Frederick Tappenden, who ran a boarding school at the house from about 1845.

The earliest buildings on the site were mentioned in 1589 and consisted of a gatehouse, malthouse and farm, all in a state of decay. In 1649 the main house had garrets over the upper floor and stood in nine acres of ground. At the end of the 17th century the house was lived in by Lord Fauconberg, whose wife Mary was Oliver Cromwell's third daughter. In the 18th century the occupants of Sutton Court were under-tenants of the Earl of Burlington and the Dukes of Devonshire.

Sutton Court was one of two Manors in Chiswick, and was known by that name as early as 1181. In the early 16th century it was owned by Sir Thomas More.

67.   This house in Sutton Lane is all that survives of the hospital and almshouses first proposed by Chaloner Chute (1595–1659), and built before 1676 for William Ashburnham, who owned the Manor of Sutton Court. It probably housed the Master of the hospital. The attached six tenements housed six poor Chiswick people. They were demolished in 1957 and Sutton Close flats now occupy their site, along with the partly demolished boundary wall. Lord Fauconberg and his wife Mary, successive owners of the Manor, left in their wills money for mourning gowns for the women in the hospital.

The area of Sutton Lane, Little Sutton House, and the almshouses was a hamlet by 1590, known as Little Sutton. It appears as a separate entry in the rate books listing eleven houses in 1795, and fourteen in 1801. On the west side of Sutton Lane were market gardens, with park land from the larger houses on the east side.

68.   Tappenden's dairy in Sutton Lane photographed in 1901. It stood opposite Little Sutton, whose porch can be seen on the left. Prior to 1886 the property was owned and lived in by the Dancer family, market gardeners, who were said to have been able to trace their ownership back to 1623. From 1886 until 1903 it was let to Mr Benjamin F. Tappenden, who was the brother-in-law of Mr Francis N. Dancer. Benjamin was the son of Frederick Tappenden, who had run a boarding school at Sutton Court. In 1914 the Tappenden family bought the property from their aunt, Mrs F. Dancer, but sold it in 1921 to United Dairies, who still use the site as a depot.

69.& 70.   Two photographs showing the garden side and the stable yard of Little Sutton, which stood at the junction of Sutton Lane with Barrowgate Road. The estate was offered for sale as building land in 1905, although the house survived until 1924. In 1928 Chiswick Garage opened on the site. Little Sutton would appear to have been built about 1791, and its first occupant to have been Lord Montraith.

In 1915 the police discovered in the house a large consignment of paintings, antiques, gold, silver and jewellery. The occupier Mr J.T. Moss and his wife Elizabeth were charged with receiving silver spoons and other items, knowing them to have been stolen. The police discovery was made in the course of prosecuting three men for being habitual criminals and taking part in a number of burglaries in Kensington, Notting Hill and Bayswater.

71.   The Queen's Head in Sutton Lane as it looked in the 1920s, when Mr Herbert Robinson was the landlord. A public house by that name, situated at Little Sutton, can be traced back to 1706.

At some time during the last century it acquired the nickname 'The Hole in the Wall' as the landlord, in order to obtain easy access across the road to his poultry and pigs, knocked a hole in the opposite wall. The present public house was built in 1925.